A Woman's Journey

Stories of Substance, Survival and Success

Paris Love & 7 Remarkable Women

BALBOA.PRESS

A DIVISION OF HAY HOUSE

Balboa Press books may be ordered through booksellers or by contacting:

Balboa Press
A Division of Hay House
1663 Liberty Drive
Bloomington, IN 47403
www.balboapress.com
1 (877) 407-4847

Because of the dynamic nature of the Internet, any web addresses or links contained in this book may have changed since publication and may no longer be valid. The views expressed in this work are solely those of the author and do not necessarily reflect the views of the publisher, and the publisher hereby disclaims any responsibility for them.

The author of this book does not dispense medical advice or prescribe the use of any technique as a form of treatment for physical, emotional, or medical problems without the advice of a physician, either directly or indirectly. The intent of the author is only to offer information of a general nature to help you in your quest for emotional and spiritual well-being. In the event you use any of the information in this book for yourself, which is your constitutional right, the author and the publisher assume no responsibility for your actions.

Any people depicted in stock imagery provided by Getty Images are models, and such images are being used for illustrative purposes only.
Certain stock imagery © Getty Images.

Scripture taken from the Holy Bible, NEW INTERNATIONAL VERSION®. Copyright © 1973, 1978, 1984, 2011 by Biblica, Inc. All rights reserved worldwide. Used by permission. NEW INTERNATIONAL VERSION® and NIV® are registered trademarks of Biblica, Inc. Use of either trademark for the offering of goods or services requires the prior written consent of Biblica US, Inc.

Print information available on the last page.

ISBN: 978-1-9822-3662-5 (sc)
ISBN: 978-1-9822-3664-9 (hc)
ISBN: 978-1-9822-3663-2 (e)

Library of Congress Control Number: 2019920258

Balboa Press rev. date: 12/10/2019

Inspire. Motivate. Educate

Table of Contents

Foreword   Jacquie Hood Martin, PhD

Part One

Part Two

Dedication

This anthology is dedicated to all the women who have come before us and those who will come after. We stand on the shoulders of our ancestors as we journey through this life, knowing we can unapologetically stand in our power. We are mothers, daughters, wives, sisters, grandmothers who walk in faith unmasked and unafraid of being the best version of ourselves.

Each story reflects how obstacles and roadblocks were conquered with faith and perseverance. We believe we must share our stories so other women can know how to step out on faith and be the woman they were meant to be.

Foreword

We are a sum total of many of the experiences we have encountered in life. Often times we do not know where those experiences will come from, yet we are led on a journey that is life-altering. Each journey we take allows us to explore more. We are in the process of becoming what we are intended to be. Stories told in this book give way to joy, pain, sorrow, heartfelt love, and desire. We hear the words all too familiar that 'there is a time and a season for everything under the sun.' However, we are never really quite prepared for our season.

Seasons catch us off-guard, can throw us into a tailspin, or simply shake our very foundation. As you embark on this wonderful reading journey, give yourself room to grow, to breathe, to forgive, to heal, to love, to listen, to learn, to be heard, to be understood, and find peace in your heart to carry on. Paris Love, and the amazing writers have compiled a simply refreshing body of work that will see you through each and every season upon which you may find yourself. On each page you may find a story that you have heard before, one that you have lived through yourself, or one that reminds you that life's moments are precious. Please do not take one single solitary moment for granted. The key to finding your footing is giving room for balance to stabilize itself in your space. We are often so in a hurry to get from point A to point B, or trying to live one grand experience after the next, that we don't allow time for the process of growth to fully run its course in our lives.

Processes takes time. Time that we often to do not want to give way to. Just think how vastly different our lives would be if we didn't rush into everything, but thought things through, counted the cost, pondered the consequences, or simply let it settle in our spirit for a little while.

Jacquie Hood Martin, PhD
Author of *Fulfilled! The Art and Joy of Balanced Living*
http://jacquiehood.com

You are far more precious than jewels
~ *Proverbs 31:10*

Part One

Truth
Paris Love

You are vulnerable when you tell your story, the story that's your truth at the moment, yet you want to be transparent, real, and it hurts to speak your reality at that moment, but you do it. After all, you have always been of integrity and truth. You hold space for others, especially when they reveal their precious moments. So, you go for it at least to get it out in the open, and you don't want others to think you are a fake. You can't be and do for everyone as you have always done. When will you get to cry, feel pain, sadness, scream, yell, or relax and take time to smell the roses, and not feel judged or guilty about it? So, you tell the pain that's your truth right now, at that very moment and it feels good to remove the mask even if deep down their perception of you changes. Who cares? This is your truth at the moment. So, you tell it, in its raw form, you don't reveal all but enough, so they understand. The goal is not for them to feel put off by your pain, only to recognize you are human and shit happens to you too. You lay the mask down with all its glory and ugliness, and for that moment, brief as it may be, you feel good. You own your shit not that you haven't in the past, but this vulnerability thing and letting others in is new to you.

You have always been the strong one, the one everyone comes to with their crap and often time without asking they dump their sadness, their pains on you. You don't internalize their stories, because it's their story and journey, but you gently hold space for them to release. But who is that person for you? You look to the left, the right, front and back. All you see are blank faces and the sound of crickets. So, who has your back? Who will not judge you? Who won't hold your shame over you as if it's a personal badge of honor? In the sea of faces, you don't recognize a single person, and your sadness grows as you know in your heart of hearts there has to be at least one person, just one, that's all you need. And this person can't be your mom or dad. Someone out there should love and cherish you for who you are, and support the good, the bad, and the ugly. At least we hope there is.

So, you do what has been done to you. You tell someone; a friend, a confidant, you are vulnerable for a moment. You tell your truth at that moment. Not to boast. Not to get sympathy, but this is what's happening at this moment. And it's been building for so long, you need to release it, or you're going to go crazy, really crazy.

You release, you feel proud of yourself, you did it!!! Until you wake up days later and realize they didn't even acknowledge your pain, your truth at that moment. And it takes you back to that dark space of being alone, again. And this is why you aren't vulnerable. Is this why you fear standing in your truth at that moment?

Did we reveal our truth at that moment to get sympathy? No. Do we want to be loved and liked by others? On a deep, deep level, we all want this, no matter the lies we tell ourselves in that we don't care what others think, that's bullshit, we do. We felt that way as children, and we certainly feel that way as adults.

Millions of thoughts run through your head. But none of it is about being liked or loved, but more about feeling shame for sharing your truth at that moment. You feel a hint of sadness for that person, how much pain and depression are they going through right now, that they couldn't at least acknowledge your truth at that moment. All you wanted was for them to say, it's going to be alright. A simple hug would have meant so much.

What's the lesson here? It's okay to be vulnerable and trust others with our deepest and darkest secrets. But we have to be mindful of who we are entrusted to hold our deepest and darkest fears. We should have a tribe of individuals who will love and support us, and we have to be able to do the same. There should only be two-way streets - one-way relationships should be avoided at all costs. Second, we have to check our motives, when we go into upset, instead of checking others, first, check yourself and see if your intentions were sound.

Aha Moment

Aha Moment

"I can do all this through him who gives me strength."

~ ~ Philippians 4:13 (NIV)

Although She Was Poor, No One Knew Her Story
Glenda Woodard

She was a tall, slender built, quiet, meek, and attractive woman with a contagious smile and gentle spirit. She was a beautician by trade and a cook by occupation. She worked as a cook, part-time, and a beautician whenever ladies in the community requested help in getting their hair straightened and curled. She was a single parent with an 8-year-old daughter. She worked hard to take care of her child. She loved her family and enjoyed helping people. There were many times when she fixed ladies hair in the community, and they didn't have the money to pay her. She would tell them to pay her later or don't worry about it. Her name was Louise, but all her friends called her Beulah. Sixty-six years ago, she smiled and thanked God, as she gave birth to a new Bundle of Joy, a baby girl! She was elated to share the joy and happiness of this special moment with her family and friends. She dated the Father of her children but never committed to marry because she felt that she was not led to do so. Oh, how proud and excited she was of her daughters! Oh, what a blessing it was to have two beautiful girls, one eight years old, named Juanita and a new baby, named Glenda!

She had lived through various trials, tribulations, and hardships. She lived in a tiny neighborhood where all the neighbors knew each other and helped each other. Louise and her children lived in the home with Louise's mother, Nelia, and other siblings. A change in the family status brought about sickness, difficulties, and other challenges. Louise's Father died from food poisoning. A brother, while on military leave from the Army, was killed. Her mother died from a severe medical illness. One sister was killed by her sister's husband; another sister died from natural causes, and another brother died from cancer. Her mother, Nelia, was a robust and faithful prayer warrior and a grandmother who never missed going to church even if she didn't feel well. Louise was a loyal prayer warrior, as well. Louise would walk around the house, in the yard or whatever she was doing, she would often pray. She would pray, "Lord, please help us to get through this day," meaning whatever challenges we face today, please help us. It was a statement included in most of her prayers. Her children were her life; she loved them, adored them, taught and raised them with love, respect, and dignity.

There were times when buying food was a challenge, but she knew the good Lord was with her and would make a way, somehow, for her to get food to feed her children and He did. She would get school clothes for her children that were placed by a dumpster to be picked up by the garbage truck. The garments were left by another family member who had little girls. Louise would wash and iron those clothes because the size was the exact size that her children could wear. Those clothes were beautiful, expensive clothes. Louise would tell Glenda that if her teachers asked her where her mother bought her clothes because they were so pretty, Glenda was to say, "I don't know." Glenda did as her mother had instructed. Glenda's teachers would often say that her mother dressed her very well, and Glenda's hair was long and braided beautifully. Louise had unwavering faith! Louise was a hard worker and always dressed very nice and neat. Her hair always looked beautiful because Louise was a beautician and could fix her hair beautifully. All though she was poor, no one knew her full story. Louise was a woman of strength and courage. She leaned on the Lord to carry her through the tough times that she faced in life. She knew to trust God because she had evidence through difficulties she had suffered in the past where God showed up, helped her, and blessed her.

Louise got pregnant with Juanita in the 12th grade. She was a star basketball player. Loved by the teachers and played extremely well. She also helped to win most basketball games. She was disappointed getting pregnant, but it never held her down. She was a motivated, determined person and worked hard to help take care of her baby girl, Juanita.

When Juanita graduated from high school, she moved to California from Alabama to live with her Uncle Daniel. That's when Uncle Daniel helped Juanita financially to go to Nursing school to get her LVN license. Juanita finished Nursing School. Her first job was as a Licensed Vocational Nurse (LVN). Juanita was able to help her mother financially and her baby sister, Glenda. Juanita would send her mother money every two weeks to pay bills and buy grocery. She helped to purchase some of Glenda's school clothing as well. This was when the living conditions for Louise was much better. Louise never considered applying for food stamps to help with the groceries because she said if she was able to work, she could buy food for her family. Louise worked as a cook in a town 25 miles away and had to catch a bus every morning at 5:00 a.m. to be at work by 6:30 a.m. The bus service in that small town was not always dependable, but Louise made it work every day that she could. Louise and her two girls lived at her mother's home with three of her brothers and a sister. It was a small four-room, three bedrooms and a kitchen and one bathroom with a total of ten people living in it, but everyone worked except Nelia and one sister. It was fun during the holidays. Every weekend when they would have fried fish that Uncle Yake had caught when he went fishing, that was at least two times a week. They had a massive garden with corn, okra, collard greens, turnip greens, field peas and snap beans. Louise and Nelia always cooked veggies from the garden, and the food was delicious. Tasty home-cooked meals with buttermilk cornbread and fried apple pies for dessert. Grandmother Nelia made the fried apple pies, and Louise would cook turnip greens and dumplings. This meal was a real treat for the family at least once or twice a month. The family would gather to eat, and it was good food and playing games (cards, checkers and dominos) throughout the day.

Juanita finished high school, went on to nursing school, and became a Licensed Vocational Nurse (LVN). She was married and was blessed with a beautiful daughter and a handsome son. Glenda was the Salutatorian of her Senior Class and graduated with high honors from high school. She went to Business College and majored in Business Administration. She married a United States Air Force Sergeant, and they had one lovely, beautiful daughter.

Glenda desperately wanted to be an Executive Secretary after graduating from high school because she was a Business major in high school. She tried very hard to get a job as a secretary, but all her efforts were unsuccessful. No matter how hard she tried to get a job as an Executive Secretary, it didn't happen. Every job interview for administrative duties required a typing score of 40 words per minute (wpm). Each time Glenda took a typing test, she scored less than 40 wpm. It made Glenda very sad because she was an excellent typist, but for some reason, she could not type 40 words per minute. She was interviewed for an Executive Secretary position at Hughs Aircraft in Los Angeles, California, but could not pass the typing test. The Supervisor who interviewed Glenda wanted to hire her and told Glenda if she didn't pass the typing test, she would not be hired for the position. Glenda passed the written test with a score of 90. She could not pass the typing test, and she couldn't understand why she got so nervous while typing until it made her fail the test. Her typing score would always be 38 wpm every time. Glenda was distraught and deeply hurt that she could not reach her goal after being so close. It had to be a reason for this happening that she did not understand but later learned that it was not in God's plan for her to be a secretary. She would pray and ask God to help her pass the typing test. She had moved to California to live with Juanita at this time, and Juanita made it a weekly task to take Glenda to apply for jobs. Glenda interviewed for several typing jobs but could not reach that passing score of 40 wpm. After several tries taking typing tests and failing them, Juanita asked Glenda to apply for a Nursing Assistant job at the same hospital she worked. Glenda didn't want a career as a Nursing Assistant, but she applied for the Nurse Assistant job anyway to please Juanita. Glenda took the test for Nursing Assistant and passed it. She was very excited! She thanked and praised God for making it happen. Now she would be able to help her mother financially to pay her bills and live more peacefully.

Glenda was trained and received a Certified Nursing Assistant

Certificate from Ranch Los Amigos Hospital in Downey, California. This was an exciting day because now she was trained and ready to work because she could help her mother financially as her sister had done. Glenda worked with Muscular Dystrophy, Polio, and Cancer patients; loved every moment of it. She married Sgt. David Woodard. After being married 11 years, she traveled to Germany and other states in the United States. Her husband, David, was assigned to a base in Mississippi, which was 317 miles from where Glenda's mother lived. They visited Louise frequently since it was only a 5-hour drive. During this time Glenda was working for the Federal Government, and her daughter Shanita was in the First Grade. Sgt, Woodard was an instructor on the Air Force base, and life was good; their life was happier than ever. They had recently spent a three-year tour in Germany, gotten use to the German culture, good food, fun times but was looking forward to returning to the United States.

On a Tuesday morning in 1986 around 4:00 a.m., Glenda received a phone call from her cousin in Birmingham, Alabama and was told that her mother had been in a car accident. Glenda immediately told David that she had to leave to go and see about her mother. David stated they should wait until the weekend when he could request leave from the Air Force, and they could drive to Alabama together. Glenda listened to her husband. But in her mind, she knew she could not wait until the weekend, so while David was at work, Glenda made a reservation at the Greyhound Bus Station. She left the following day, without her husband's permission to see about her mother. Glenda caught a cab to go to the bus station that Wednesday morning. As the cab was leaving the housing area, David was entering the neighborhood coming home on his lunch break. When Glenda saw David's car, she slid down in the back seat of the cab so that David could not see her. She had left a long letter attached to the refrigerator explaining to David why she had to leave without him. She apologized to him for not coordinating the leave, but she knew that it was crucial to see about her mother. She had talked to other family members and was told that the hospital her mother was taken to had diagnosed her mother with a spinal cord injury, which was causing her mother not to be able to stand, use her legs, or use her arms.

Louise had developed quadriplegia from being hurt in the car accident. She was paralyzed from her neck down to her feet. Her mother was later blessed to regain movement and feeling in her arms and legs after being in rehabilitation, but she could not walk without using a walker.

Glenda moved her mother to Mississippi to live with her family for three months and later moved Louise to an assisted Living Facility, five minutes from where Glenda lived. During the time Louise lived with Glenda and her family, Louise would tell Glenda, she couldn't believe that she knew how to bath her in bed, turning her from side to side. Glenda would change her bed linen and so many other things by herself. Glenda would say, it was because she was trained how to take care of a sick patient who was not able to take care of themselves. Louise would smile and say, well, all I can say is, you know what you are doing because after you bathe me, I sure do smell mighty good! They would both get a good laugh from that!

Juanita, who lived in California, had been diagnosed with diabetes and was not able to help take care of their mother. She was sick herself; therefore, Glenda, traveled from Mississippi to Alabama frequently to be the Caregiver for their mother before moving Louise to Mississippi. Going back and forth from Mississippi to Alabama became very tiring. Glenda had a family, worked 95 to 100 hours every two weeks, and because of the demands of her job, the traveling was becoming stressful due to the illness she had.

Louise did not understand why Juanita never came to Mississippi to help with her care. She later accepted it and prayed about it, but as a mother, she just couldn't understand why her older daughter didn't come to visit and help care for her. Louise loved both of her daughters and was deeply hurt, not knowing why this was happening. She knew Juanita loved her but the question of why she never came to visit or call, Louise did not understand and neither did Glenda. Louise knew the Lord was with her, even at a time when her younger daughter was her only Caregiver. No one knew that Juanita was sick at the same time Louise was ill. Juanita's daughter later informed Glenda that Juanita was in the hospital. Juanita's diabetes was out of control, and she was very sick. Juanita loved her mother dearly and wanted to help her mother, but she couldn't because of her illness. She knew she would visit her mother once she was cured of diabetes; therefore, she suffered in silence, alone. Glenda never told Louise Juanita was ill because that would have devastated Louise. When Juanita's illness became worse, she notified her daughter to come to help her. Juanita was always driven to excel in whatever challenge she faced, but this was one time she needed help from her daughter. She was beautiful, smart, and motivated, but now she knew God was in control of her health and that her life was in God's hands. By this time, Glenda had moved on to a successful career but was diagnosed with a muscle disease called Polymyositis. With God's help, her health improved, and she was promoted through the ranks. Not as an Executive Secretary, but as a Financial Management Officer working with the Department of Defense in the United States Air Force. She managed and executed the Operations and Maintenance and Reserve Appropriation Budgets that totaled over $100M for an Air Force Installation.

While Glenda was enjoying her new promotion, she was still committed to caring for their mother. On Dec 19, 1996, in Mississippi, Louise was admitted into the hospital, and one day later, Juanita was admitted in the hospital on Dec 20, 1996, in California. Louise and Juanita's health seemed to improve during the next week, but later it would get worse, during the same time. Glenda and her niece, Valerie, talked daily about their mother's health. They were in total shock as to how both mother's health improved and declined at the same time. They could not explain it because it was a situation where God's hand could be seen so vividly into their mother's illness and care.

Louise passed-on to be with the Lord on Jan 2, 1997, and one day later, Jan 3, 1997, Juanita passed-on to be with the Lord.

My mother and my sister are together in heaven after not being able to be together on earth during the last days of their illness. Our mother's broken heart was mended together by God. When her older daughter, Juanita, meets her mother, Louise, in heaven; what a glorious celebration this must have been.

Now I understood why it was not in God's plan for me to be an

Executive Secretary. I had to be a Nurse Assistant to learn how to take care of my sick mother.

I am so thankful that I was obedient to follow God's plan rather than my idea.

God's excellent plan beautifully designs our lives!

> *Jeremiah 29:11 (NIV) – For I know the plans I have for you, declares the Lord, "plans to prosper you and not to harm you, plans to give you hope and a future.*

My Prayer:

Father God, empowered by your Spirit and keeping my eyes stayed on you, I have learned on this journey that your plan for me is eternal. One, through obedience, that will help me live in peace, joy, and happiness. Thank you for blessing me to have beautiful memories of my dear loving mother and beautiful sister. The love we shared will remain in my heart until we are joined together in glory with our Lord and Savior, Jesus Christ.

Aha Moment

Aha Moment

"Consider it pure joy, my brothers and sisters, whenever you face trials of many kinds, 3 because you know that the testing of your faith produces perseverance. 4 Let perseverance finish its work so that you may be mature and complete, not lacking anything."
~ ~ James 1:2-4 (NIV)

Four Years- Forever Changed
Georgia Day

My first ten years of life were spent in a small town, about an hour from Houston, TX. I was in the same elementary school during this time, with teachers, my brother and sister had had, and I loved it. I had lots of friends I had known for many years. We were very close to the water and had an old rambling country home, surrounded by lots of neighbors in the area. While we had a shale driveway, outside our property, the streets were paved. (this would change in a big way later.)

My mother's parents lived in Oklahoma, and I spent every summer with them, from the time I was three years old. There was very little difference in routine during these years. One day, my brother told me we were moving, so I asked my parents about it. They said that we were moving at the end of the school year and I could not say anything about it until they told me I could. Toward the end of the school year, the 5th grade for me, I heard many conversations on the bus from other kids, and I knew I had not said anything. I told my parents, and they then said it was ok for me to say "yes" when people asked me. I had led such a comfortable and consistent life and had no clue what the move would mean for me. On the last day of school that year, my parents and brother picked me up from school, and we headed for southern Louisiana. At the same time, my older sister left for her first year of college in Mississippi. I had always had her close to me at home, and this was quite a shock.

My father, who had been in the insurance business in Houston, had bought a large farm and prepared to grow crops and raise cattle. He hated the rat race and had always wanted to live and work in the country. I remember during the summer, we stayed at a motel because our house was being built. I had no idea where we were, and the culture shock was just the beginning. My first trip out to our property took us off the main highway and onto a dirt road with cattle guards (this is a series of connected, equally spaced pipes that cattle cannot cross). The house was about 2 miles from the main highway, and there were acres of crops being grown. Walking into the house, I did see some familiar furniture and my bedroom was large enough so that my sister, who had left for college, could have a place to stay when she came home from college to visit. I had had a massive collection of stuffed animals that I loved having on my bed, and there were none in the new house. The kitchen was tiny, and there was no garage, which we had always had.

The first summer passed quickly, and before I knew it, it was time for school to start. I dreaded going to a new school, a private Catholic school, when my first five grades had been in a public school. I was unprepared for the Cajun way of life. They were a close-knit, verbal, happy, affectionate people, sharing their life stories in their French/English dialect, over informal, large meals; whereas, conversations in our home were not to ever be repeated outside the home unless given permission. Generally, the people in this area were almost always dressed casually. I had always seen my dad in a suit before and seeing him in khaki shirt and pants as he took us to school and picked us up was a shock as well. I did not understand half of what the kids were saying (heavy dialect), the classrooms were primitive (compared to what I had been used to), and everyone was Catholic. I will never forget the first day I was in the cafeteria in line, and the server was asking the kids if they wanted "dirty rice." I had no idea what it was but took some anyway. I had one bite and left the rest, thinking that they meant the rice was dirty, and it did have black and brown specks in it. Many years later I found out that it had sausage, chicken livers and bell pepper in it.

As kids usually do, I adapted as well as I could. My parents became friends with a couple in a larger town who had several children, and we began to attend church with them. Having been raised in the Episcopal

Church, I once again was not prepared for the shock of a Catholic service, which at that time was conducted in Latin. Thankfully, the following year, my brother and I transferred to a larger, more modern Catholic school in that town, and I began to make some friends.

I remember the nights scared me; our house was about one-tenth the size of our previous home, and there was little soundproofing. I would lay awake and listen to the owls hooting and the coyotes howling at the full moons. One of the bright spots was the pool my parents built, and I enjoyed swimming until I had company – snakes. There was a pond about 100 yards from the pool so that the water moccasins would slide right in at will. Each time I was out for a swim when this happened, my parents were out of town, so our baby sitter and I killed the snakes. I learned to make a detailed inspection of the water before I got in after that. One year, the entire state had a rat infestation. I had been in my parent's bedroom one night, returned to my room, only to find a mouse on my pillow. Of course, my screaming brought my Dad running, and he dispatched the mouse.

During this time, my brother decided to join the Navy, so after he left, I became an only child. We lived so far out in the country that I had to have kids spend the weekend with me, or I spent the weekend with them. I was finally adapting to the change in most ways. However, during the time we lived there, we had hurricanes every year, and the crops failed time after time. I remember several times, we could not get any cars out of the property, due to colossal rainfall. One time, we were going to go shopping, and my mother was dressed up and in heels. We got on Dad's tractor, hoping to get out, but got stuck. I still remember my Mother taking off her heels and walking in the mud back to the house.

My parents had to make some decisions about their future and mine. They, in middle age, decided to both begin new careers, sold the farm, and we moved to Austin, TX. My dad became a real estate home builder, and my mother became an interior designer. I spent that last Louisiana summer with my grandparents, and they drove me to our new home. We were now in a city with neighbors, two of whom became close friends over time, and our house was two-story, with an attached garage.

My bedroom was upstairs, and unless my brother was home visiting, I had space to myself. My mother had an office upstairs, but she was usually not up there at night. I slowly began to feel connected, as much as a teenager can, and was happy and loved my new area.

The four years spent in Louisiana had a profound impact on me. I learned about different cultures, a different way of life, and adapting as the only child at home. I realized later how beautiful the Cajun culture is – when they decide you are a friend, you are a friend for life! I was exposed to some of the best cooking in the world. And, as much as I dislike change, this experience prepared me for many more changes to come in my life, not the least of which was retiring from government service, selling our home and living and working across the US for ten years in an RV! Would I live in the country again? I told my husband before we got married that I only had a couple of issues – the primary one being that I would never move to the country again! Throughout our 34+ years of marriage, he has always kept that promise.

Aha Moment

Aha Moment

"The question isn't who's going to let me. It's who is going to stop me."
~ Ayn Rand

How Growth Within Led to Growth Without
Angela I. Schutz

*I*n 2009 I became very interested in the self-development movement. It was clear to me that my life was all about surface and tangible elements. I rarely looked within to try to figure out why I did the things I did. I was deeply committed to the concept of being "the best" in all areas of my life. It never occurred to me that in my quest for being "the best," I was putting up a wall between myself and others who felt I was untouchable. I am a coach. Mostly a Career Coach, but I am also certified as a Life Coach, a Dream Coach, an NLP practitioner, and a Myers-Briggs Administrator.

As you can see, getting certified in many venues was my attempt to be the best at what I did, and, of course, I was showing the world that I had credibility. What I was not showing the world was that I am a real human being with deep feelings and passions about the work I do and about life, in general. What I gave up by wanting to be "the best" was the ability to connect with others on a soul level. How could "the best" coach relate to the problems and concerns of the average person? After all, wasn't it implicit that the coach who was "the best" was beyond all the trials and tribulations of life?

I was oblivious to that message for many years. I had created a coaching business, but it was just limping along. I was lucky to have five clients a year, and since the Career Coaching business is one where clients should move through the process to land jobs and never, or at least not for many years, need the service again. The entire time my business was limping along trying to remain solvent, I was delving into all sorts of training by the top people in the self-development movement. I studied with Jack Canfield, Marcia Weider, Debra Poneman, and Marci Shimoff. I took courses, attended webinars, listened to podcasts, and attended Mastermind groups. Each year I developed more and more skills, and yet, the coaching business kept limping along.

I was trying everything! Every time I was exposed to a new name, I bought the program, listened to the cd, or took the online course. I did The Work by Byron Kadee, I joined Your Year of Miracles and Yes to Success. I listened to and read everything by Brene Brown. I loved it all and learned so much. I wouldn't have traded this path for anything!

And yet, I was still hiding behind the wall of "greatness." What was it that would help me just to be myself? How could I open up and let others in to see the real me? The burning question was always: What was I afraid others would see in me that would drive them away?

Years had gone on. I had lots of valuable knowledge, but my finances were at rock bottom, and then my husband of 43 years died. His death wasn't as hard to deal with as the surprise, or rather sucker punch, he left me. After he died, I found out that he had cashed out his retirement and spent it on himself or someone else, he had so little life insurance that it wasn't enough to bury him, and (are you ready for this because I wasn't!) he left $60,000 worth of debts that I had to pay!

It was funny how any sense of mourning I might have felt, went right out the window! I knew that I was not going to let this stop me or cause me to lose the home I had lived in for 43 years. I knew I would have to suck it up and get moving. I also had no idea where to begin to attack these problems. How could the one who always looked like she had a perfect life ask for help? How could she let this happen to her? I had no idea! I only had the resolve to make it right and being a businesswoman myself, albeit perhaps a poor example of one, I knew I would pay off every penny owed to other businesses. I would not ignore the responsibility to pay these debts, yet, here I was faced with the problem of "how to eat the elephant"!

Now, right about now, you may be thinking, "that poor woman." If this had been your story, I would be feeling very sorry for you. For your loss and all your struggles - but wait! There's more.

Shortly after my husband died, I began to have some strange symptoms that something was medically wrong with me. My hands began to go numb, so numb that if I tried to put something in the oven, I couldn't hold onto it, and dropped whatever it was all over the floor. I could no longer wear earrings because I couldn't feel my fingertips. I began searching for answers. I went to my doctor and was put through a battery of tests. She then sent me to a neurologist who put me through more tests. It took eight months for them to discover I had a considerable growth inside my spinal column that was pinching my nerves. One of the problems was that this growth was between disc one and two, which is an area in your body that controls your heart, your lungs, and your extremities. Pretty serious stuff!

I was sent to the best spinal surgeon at Yale. He kept shaking his head and telling me that I was dealt a lousy hand of cards! He would also add that without surgery, I would be dead or paralyzed in about two months. All of the blood vessels that led to my brain were wrapped around the growth! The surgical outcome looked bleak.

But wait! Isn't this supposed to be an anthology about triumph? Well, that is what it is! The surgeon was extremely skillful and extremely creative because unlike any other person on this planet, I have in my head and neck a metal plate, a bone from my pelvis for additional strength, two fused discs, two metal rods, and three bolts, all to hold my head on! The good news is that although I have lost some movement when trying to turn my head from side to side, I do not look like a zombie! I am also completely able to walk and move freely to do everything I need to do. But this isn't the end of my story!

What the physical growth within me gave me as a gift was tremendous growth as a person. I have learned the value of vulnerability. Having to struggle so much to learn to walk and move again taught me how to ask for what I needed rather than say: "I'm fine." I am so much more open to everyone's struggles, whether it be in finding a new job or living a good life. Today, I am teaching two college courses, running a woman's group called: Dream Dare Dance, and coaching over 30 clients! I am grateful for every day and happily dating. I now have a charmed life filled with love, gratitude, and triumph.

Aha Moment

Aha Moment

Aha Moment

"If we don't change, we don't grow. If we don't grow, we aren't really living."

~ ~ *Gail Sheehy*

Separation Anxiety
Kimberly Sharkey

*H*ow much one decision will cost?

Who would have thought the image of family would advertently be pulled right from under my feet by my own? I mean, I fell flat on my face to end up learning how to stand up and leaning on an unbalanced table. It was like a scene out of the Matrix movie fighting a battle in slow motion. Time was ticking and life became a big old experience to be figured out and not just lived. The fight for normalcy was a silent battle and my security in independence was a joke. It all started when my parents decided to separate.

I know I was too young to understand, but as I got older. I later questioned, "If my parents would have known the consequences of their decision, would they have changed their mind?" Their marital status cost me an emotional roller coaster ride I didn't stay in line for. This wasn't a "Fun Town" (Chicago's Finest Theme Park in the 70s), kind of ride. The uncertainty of my childhood development was unsteady. I struggled with connecting with others where it appeared to be the normal to live in a single parent household in my community, when I knew what it was like to have both of my parents.

Our household stood on the value of **loving your family** and sticking together no matter what. We had food on the table, a roof over our head and clothes on our back and that is how my parents demonstrated their love, then in a matter of their decision, it became divided. You would think someone would have considered the plague of a child, but instead I experienced lack and learning how to survive.

When I was five or six years old, my mother decided to separate from her husband. That was probably the last time I heard the term "husband" until my adulthood. I grew up in a neighborhood where both of my parents' mothers lived approximately 5 minutes away, so being with family was a norm for me. My uncles and aunts lived on the same street, so my cousins were nearby and we were together constantly. We had family reunions, birthday celebrations, holiday dinners and seasonal barbeques that we now no longer participated in because of the divide. I didn't know family would take sides or rather not get involved in such a covenant. By the age of eight or nine, my family was estranged. It was challenging to visit cousins as the separation and later divorce became "the way of family" in my community.

My father visited at any our short-lived living quarters. We had now lived in Altgeld Gardens, Robert Taylors, on the West and East Side and spent some time in the Low End to name a few places around Chicago. All during my grammar school years. I was constantly uprooted by having to attend a different school and having to make new childhood friends on what it seemed every year. By eighth grade, I've been to approximately 6 different schools and each school system were teaching something different. Either I was catching up on a lesson or was honorable ahead of the class.

It was uncomfortable to embrace other relationships with the understanding that relationships can end with a blink of an eye because of my firsthand experience with my own family. When I made a friend, it was anguish to connect because I did not know how long it should last; how much time should I put into the relationship or what should they get to know about me and me them. Moreover, when we did disconnect for whatever reason I experienced anxiety. I felt like we should not have indulged in getting to know one another because the END was soon to come based on the decisions of someone else.

I felt so removed, we did not keep a home phone, so to consider getting a phone number was not a thought I initiated to keep in touch. Our number always changed; therefore, consistency was not a part of my mantra. I sensed I did not have any control over my life or the relationships I was building. I had no one to talk too. I had to fend for my life on my own, by making sense out of what was happening around me with no guidance or instructions.

Later to learn that other classmates and neighborhood kids were in similar situations, but no one helped us navigate through these changing times. As a child, we didn't have the words to formulate our expressions. In addition, for that matter neither did the adults around us. Counseling was not a word used unless you were crazy or something was wrong with you. If we saw a man at the school with a student, you could see the admiration as it was truly something to respect. We assumed. It was their father.

Then, one of the most perplexing exchanges of engagement was watching my parents interact with their significant other. Someone, who they now treated like they once treated one another. Relationships, family and any form of vulnerability or connection where all trivial for me. I didn't want to attach myself to anyone. The idea of building relationships was an illusion. My thoughts kept lingering telling me that it was all going to end anyway. I wanted to see just how it was going to end, before it even started good.

My mom did not lack having a mate or someone to talk to it seems. When one man was headed out the front door another one was coming through the back. I didn't know where she found the time to find these men. Their presence in our household gave a false security. It did not feel any more secure but more defenseless and alone with my emotions. I only felt protected by my dad there was investment in our relationship. His siblings were my uncles and aunts and they had children who were my cousins. Where were they?

I know they had some type of feeling for my mother, but our environment was not the same. I missed hearing the authority in my dad's voice. These men could not say anything to me, they did not know me like this and I would not share with them how I was feeling. However, my mom appeared to be okay with the arrangements made. Her and her significant other fought, made up and acted as if nothing happened the next day. It was chaotic, while remembering hearing my biological dad telling me at one point. "What happens in this house, stays in this house?"

After about two years of living without my father; he finally introduced me to a woman, who had children almost around the same age as me and my siblings. This was when the picture of family shattered my comprehension. I was the oldest of 4 and I didn't know how my siblings were coping. Especially when the lady's children called my father, "DAD! What was I to say? I was trying to understand this myself. Did he have other children? Was this the reason my parents separated?

About the time I became a teenager, I decided to go to the same high school as my parents when they were teenagers for a sense of connection. Only to find out that my father's girlfriend children would be walking down the same hallway as I did. One of girls wanted to act as if we were "sisters", but I had a sister and the irony was they were tall too. "No", I'm not in agreement with this type of relationship. "You are not my sister, your mom and dad aren't even married, or were they? This girl had the best of my world, my dad. I often wondered what it was like to go home at this age to a dad. Envy rose and I trusted the reasons to not like her for no reasons of her own. Did they share their day with him? Did he give them lunch money for tomorrow?

While in college, which he drove me my first year. What a memory we created. This opened the door for me to write him letters to share how I felt and my concerns as a child, but he would respond with a paragraph then signing, Love Dad. Those two words gave me a glimpse of security; however, I needed more words. Only to be told that men don't communicate like women. I did the same with my mom, but her letters would give me the responsibility to seek out my own truth, because she had her own challenges to endure.

It wasn't until college, when I was able to get a foretaste of clarity on what actually transpired between my parents. I was old enough to ask questions, not directly but enough to inquire. This is where I learned that, communication and trust is the foundation of any relationship. When I did have my first "real" boyfriend I didn't know if I should introduce him to the family or not? I wondered what kind of advice they would give us because what they initially taught me I didn't see. Adults would say, "Do as I say, not as I do." That was tough.

One thing I can say I have learned – as a growing adults was that "experiences were not our best teacher". Reflection of those experiences were. I knew it was not my parent's intent to dismantle the structure of family, but as they say, "hurt people, hurt people" and if it's not even intentional. I didn't jump into romantic relationships. It took me a while to know how to relate to a person in that manner. Yet, as a maturing adult; I believed that, if my parents attended counseling sessions then maybe they would have been able to maneuver through the hurt of what happened in their relationship. But counseling wasn't a soothing reconciliation method back then. Even a life coach would have been valuable in assisting them navigate through their parental responsibility to train their children up to have healthy relationships.

The revelation through all this for me was not to make my parents issues, my issue. I looked forward to the time when I would be able to create my original picture of family. I joined a church especially after a sermon about generational curses and from there I immerged in the studies of what it means to God about family. The dreams I yearned for my life was going to require me to pursue them, despite the blurry family structure I experienced, the need for acceptance from them, while seeking out the truth on how to deal with my separation anxiety.

I had to create my own sense of family and create my own support system with great understanding. I had to understand that people come into our lives for a reason, season or for a life lifetime. Once I was able to put that into perspective I became grateful to know that I NEEDED people but not to depend on them for my ever-evolving growth.

Aha Moment

Aha Moment

"The way we treat our children directly impacts what they believe about themselves."
~ ~ Ariadne Brilt

Innocence
Monica Fletcher

When I was a little girl, I loved dolls, good music, racing in made-up marathons, chewing bubble gum and you could easily find me climbing a barb-wire fence or two while catching lighting-bugs but the best part of my day, annoying the heck out of my baby sister! Yep, life was pretty complete and straightforward for this chick, but then our protector abruptly moved out, and all of those happy moments turned into fear. Even heard a voice once say, your parents were so happy before you were born. Then that childhood transgression took place, and the rest of my premature feelings went right on out the door! We had a dozen sleepovers at their house, and for the life of me, I still can't figure out why she chose that particular night to touch me under those covers in that way. I didn't know how to tell anyone. I didn't know what to say. I wasn't even sure what happened so why tell my momma and risk getting in trouble? I often wonder if someone did the same thing to her. I didn't know. Besides, after dad left ma had a lot on her plate, so I refused to make her sadder (that's how a child may think about his/her troubles). My mind went so far left that I began to secretly criticize myself all the time. Keep in mind; I was barely a pre-teen at this point.

My skin wasn't dark enough; the size of my face looked funny, my hair was too thick, my eye color looked weird, even the nail on my right baby toe started a debate. And of course, my figure was never quite good enough for my peers, especially to boys. Those messed-up images stayed with me throughout elementary and middle school, oh but no worries,

I learned how to mask it good by the time I reached high school. Trust me popular girls got issues too! Keeping all that stuff bottled up may have triggered my childhood seizures, and I caught the doggone flu every year for Christmas. Had to lay on the couch while my family put up the tree and decorations. I got moodier as time went on, even church felt like a chore, and that was one of my favorite places to go. I became a terrible liar and that ole stank butt attitude of mine got worse as my bruised heart continued to age. I walked around angry and aggravated when day moved slowly and if night came too soon. Between my dad leaving, the neighbor unsolicited touches, moms necessary work hours, the illnesses, the suicide attempt, and the untimely death of a friend, I felt emotionally beat-up before I turned 19 years old. Folks didn't talk much about mental health back then, 'remember baby what goes on in this house stays in this house. I also think a lot of my 'bad behavior get chalked up to, 'you just trying to be grown.' That's what the ole folks use to say about immaturity.

I never gave anyone the opportunity to ask me if I was ok and I hide my brokenness for a lot of years. The night before I left home, the voice in my dream said, you know she's never going to let you grow up,' me and my mom had a pretty bad argument earlier that day. All of those negative words seeped right on into my subconscious. Funny thing, not one word of joy or laughter did I speak or chose to hear. The voice never acknowledged the way we use to run around the house as a family, cleaning from top to bottom while singing and dancing to music. Nope, it only reminded me of all the disagreements we had. It was like watching my own two-hour drama series. So, I packed a suitcase and left the next morning after my family went to church. I was sitting at my boyfriend's apartment in tears by the time they found out. We eventually reconnected long enough for my parent to come and repossess my car. I know they were angry and embarrassed by my decision but I was stuck in a place of feeling like I would never be allowed to grow up if I stayed. Being a upstanding church kid started to feel like a lot of work!

My boyfriend was a few years older than me and in no way did he jump to say my decision was right, but I do appreciate he at least listened to my side of the story. He never made me feel like I was the devil. We did what we had to do to adjust to my new season. He grew up as a church kid to so during our time together, he worked tirelessly to pull the best back out of me, but my frustration was stuck like glue. It finally ended when my party life caught up with us. I'll never forget the night he said, "it's time for me to let you go find your way." Deep down I knew he was right so after a few years of us living together in our own place he moved out.

Almost missed high school graduation, had terrible sex for the first time, lost a lot of good friends, disrespected my parents and even reached a point where I thought I should die, nearly died as a child but my grandmother's prayers brought me back to life. I stole bubble gum when I was a kid. Shot at, almost raped twice, should've been arrested more than once for DUI, shifted through boy-toys like I was a guy, faced arrest for bounced checks, cheated with a married man. But then I made amends with my family, got my own place, forgave myself for allowing the abuse, started writing again, found a new career, ended up in the ATL, partied my butt off, dated for a while, married a new man, finished my college degree, rededicated my life to the Lord and the church. I lost a lot of weight both inside and out. Got a life coach, reconnected with a few old high school friends, still got a few trials and tribulations. (Refer to John 16:33) I forgave my dad for leaving and the girl for what she did to me. More importantly I forgive that little hurt girl inside of me too. She tries to creep up from time to time, but I am quick to let her know it's ok now because I've let those things go.

Aha Moment

Aha Moment

"Children are mirrors, they reflect back to us all we say and do."
~ ~ Pam Leo

The Journey — Back to Me
Brittany Lorenzi

"Be what you want, but always be you." – Brittany Thompson, age 17

This quote is a motto I created for my senior yearbook photo. It is one I am very passionate about, however somewhere along the way; I lost sight of it.

Growing up in a family where both of my parents owned their own companies and invested in real estate, I knew to be an entrepreneur was in my blood — having the opportunity (although at the time, I considered it more of a chore). To physically work renovating the historic buildings and seeing first-hand what it was like to run a commercial building, alongside their daily companies, allowed me to see both the benefits and hard work/risk associated with working for yourself. I loved that my parents could "take off" two weeks during the holidays every year. However, seeing them respond to business/building emergencies 24/7 and going to a baby sitter before and after school, each day wasn't quite as much fun.

During college, my parents provided me the opportunity to "do with what I saw fit" a lot behind their buildings. The only caveat was that I had to split whatever profits that might be generated with my older sister. I was so excited and immediately decided to create a small S-Corp and create a parking lot for the building tenants. As this opportunity grew, I decided to look further into ways to generate revenue from the tenants. I obtained financing and was able to provide vending/refreshment services to the building. This venture allowed me to pay for my social activities in college while providing me real-life experience to test my entrepreneurial spirit. I ended up winning a State of Indiana Collegiate Entrepreneurship Award for my business.

After college, I relocated to Cincinnati and worked for a small family-owned company redeveloping historic buildings in Over the Rhine. Once again, this experience allowed me to witness how many hats you must wear as a small business owner. It also grew my passion for redeveloping and investing in real estate.

By way of marriage and my husband received a job offer to relocate, we found ourselves in Nashville. At the time, surprisingly, redevelopment wasn't on the radar for many in Nashville. And those brave enough to consider it weren't yet looking to hire anyone. Since our anticipated stay for my husband's job training program was only two years and not much was going on in the redevelopment world. I settled for a job in commercial real estate, taking about five steps back from my role in Cincinnati. This was the first time I feel I strayed off my intended path or against, "Always Be You."

During that job, I met a lot of great people and did gain a broader knowledge in the commercial real estate world. Working for others in a more corporate, rigid environment just didn't fit with who I was or who I wanted to be. It also reinforced that I didn't want to ever work for anyone else but myself. Since the stint was to be short, I worked hard every day. I quickly established value both operationally and organizationally. Soon after, I was recognized for my strengths and allowed co-founding and helping create a new company. I would handle the business operations, and my partners (all commercial real estate brokers) would be the sales team. I was given a blank canvas and got the opportunity to create everything from the ground up collectively. The challenge of researching and figuring out the strategy and best practices was very fulfilling. Our business model was continually evolving as we grew, and the landscape of our industry changed. As we grew from 6 to 10 to 35 employees, new challenges presented themselves. One of the hardest obstacles to work through was the downturn in the economy and the commercial real estate industry as a whole. Eventually, we grew to the point where we were ready to hire a CEO to focus on Business Development. Not an area of my strength. This was key to strengthening our business development opportunities.

The company continued to grow; however, the creative and strategic side of my role started to diminish. With 75 employees and multiple locations, we were much more of a streamlined corporation than a small entrepreneurial company. Once again, I started feeling like I was getting away from who I was and what type of company I wanted to lead. After giving 110% to grow the company to where it was, often putting the business before my family, I realized the passion was gone. My role had become one of which did not match who I was. My entrepreneurial spirit had been lost. I was struggling each day by being surrounded by a team of great people and a steady paycheck and not being fulfilled because I was no longer able to be me. After meeting with Janet Walls (a fabulous executive coach at Delta Blvd), taking the Strengths Finders assessment and having several long discussions with my husband, I knew I had once again lost my way. I am the creative, forward-thinking, strategic person. My role had become rigid, black, and white and very historical thinking. I knew that I needed a change. As scary as it was, I knew I needed to get back to being me and realign my priorities in life. So, I took the step and jumped out of the window without a parachute.

I have often been asked why I didn't launch something new before I left. Now that really wouldn't have been me. There is no way I could have given 110% to my current company and my new company, so I jumped. Then I spent time thinking and renewing my focus on my priorities in life, especially my family. I felt free and so much like me again. It was the first time in 11 years my kids weren't going to school or camp from 7 am - 6 pm. Leaving what was so familiar and secure and jumping into the unknown was scary yet freeing. I didn't know what was next, but I knew that I wanted to start another venture, and I was ready for my next challenge. My entrepreneurial spirit was once again sparked. At this point, a good friend encouraged me to not focus as much on the destination, but "Enjoy the Journey" along the way. I am thankfully reminded of this with the bracelet she gave me with this theme etched on the top. To this day, I find comfort in wearing it when I feel lost in my path.

So, as I begin down my next path, while not entirely satisfied where it will take me, I know I'm ready for the journey. My passion to help others start and grow their own companies and begin their journey to what's next for them and help make their dreams a reality is extremely fulfilling. I am thankful that I am now able to help others be who they want to be, and I am again living my high school quote,

"Be What You Want, But Always Be You." I am a wife, a mother, an entrepreneur, a professional woman, but most importantly, I am me!

Aha Moment

Aha Moment

"*Success is a journey, not a destination. The doing is often more important than the outcome.*"

~ ~ *Arthur Ashe*

Breaking Cycles: Brokenness and Abuse
Lequvia K. Ousley

One of the hardest and best decisions of my life was leaving an unhealthy, abusive environment. I've shared this before in conversation amongst friends and a few family members, and I would like to share again here. I was raised in a sheltered environment in the small, rural city of Dawson, GA, a situation where I witnessed verbal, emotional, and physical abuse between my parents. I experienced verbal, emotional, and mental abuse from loved ones. I would later learn that violence is a common factor within both sides of my family, but no one talked about the effects over the years. Those familial, generational effects would later determine my views on relationships (personal and professional) and negatively shape my experiences. From those experiences, I viewed the family as the enemy. I didn't trust anyone who shared the same blood as me. What's even sadder is that I was taught to be that way from a young age. Everyone that knew me from school knew that I wasn't allowed to have company or be around anyone except my immediate family, which consisted of myself, my mother, father, and older sister. Eventually, that tight-knit family would be reduced due to my parents' separation later on.

As I grew into my teen years, naturally, writing, music, magazines, and movies became my friends. I also found myself getting lost in my favorite books. Even though I accepted Christ at the age of 10, I didn't always draw to Him for inspiration. My inspiration came from my favorite celebrities. In my mind, I believed that since they didn't know me personally, they couldn't hurt me. Sad, right? I had a few people in my life who I associated with, but I only saw them at school or talked with them by phone so my time alone in my room was great for me. There was no pressure to be something that I wasn't, and I felt free. But I was still caged within my surroundings and at times, caged within my mind, always daydreaming and envisioning myself somewhere else. I truly understood, Maya Angelou's, infamous book, "I Know Why the Caged Bird Sings." That's exactly how I felt — caged with nowhere to go. I use to make jokes with my friends, that I was "Celie" in "The Color Purple," "Precious," "Antwon Fisher," and so on and so on. I saw myself within those characters, which later inspired me to step out and move forward.

As time went on, I went to college and met people. I spent my first three years at home (I attended Darton College, a 2-year college, and later transferred to Albany State University, a 4-year university). Then, I decided to live on campus my senior year (due to the class load and problems at home). Being in that environment was even worse because there was no accountability and, in my mind, I finally had freedom. I made good grades, but I still found myself in situations that were no good, and I felt that I needed to date someone to feel "normal." I would later learn that randomly dating someone is so dull. I desired instead to be courted for marriage. Honestly, I've always believed that being "abnormal" is normal, lol (not giving in to peer pressure, being set apart from worldly pleasures, having crazy faith in the unseen, etc.). I can remember dating briefly in high school, but it wasn't anything serious. I took the situation seriously, but of course, it was all a game to them and a just another void-filler for me. I will never forget the words my mother said to me when I had a bad attitude one day: "If you want attention, you better find it in that boy." That was death to my self-esteem, and another door opened for more problems later — problems I experienced because I allowed them to happen. Eventually, I hated being by myself. Since 1998 (8th grade), I battled anxiety after my parents separated and ultimately divorced. Writing in my journal was still my saving grace at the time. In 2005 (sophomore year in college) my anxiety turned into social anxiety.

The anxiety caused me to not sleep at night (I purposely stayed up to avoid nightmares), bad eating habits (eating too less or overeating), depression, and just fearful of life and anything good happening for myself. I believed every negative word spoken over myself and all that I was seeing around me. My relationship with my mother wasn't the best, and my relationship with my father eventually resurfaced in Jan. 2008.

Words are powerful, and it is so important to know your worth as a person. As I look back, I realized that because of what I saw as a child, that's how I viewed relationships. I lived out those words that were spoken over me. As a young woman, I had a responsibility to know my worth. Even though I decided to leave my family physically, I still found myself in unhealthy relationships with others and mentally processing negative emotions. I allowed myself to endure name-calling, false accusations, mind-games, manipulation, and constant disrespect just for the sake of having a relationship. I even encountered a situation where my privacy was invaded, and I became angry and physical with the other person. That's when I became scared. Scared of myself and who I had become. I didn't know who to trust anymore, and I was afraid of being an abusive person. I realized that I needed help and that I can't continue to place myself in unhealthy situations. From those experiences, I knew I had to make some serious decisions to gain freedom once again.

My livelihood and worth are more important than being with people who don't value me as a person. Today, I'm so happy to know Jesus Christ as my Savior. Even though I didn't always acknowledge Him, He tugged on my heart so many times to remove myself from those situations. My many prayers and moments of crying out for help were not in vain. Throughout my teen and young adult years, I kept a journal filled with inspirational quotes and scriptures and Psalms 27 was a scripture I referenced a lot amid trials. Ever since I made that one decision to leave an abusive environment on January 5, 2008, the Lord has been faithful. I admit it wasn't a natural choice because I struggled with my emotions. My family was all I knew. I also knew that there had to be a better life for me in store than what

I was seeing. Being in God's will was more important for my soul, sanity, and well-being. And the Lord has kept me through it all. He provided for me when I lacked, allowed Godly relationships to be formed, pushed me out of my comfort zone, and just simply loved me where I was. He continuously loves me unconditionally even when I mess up or when I find myself dealing with someone who is not graceful or merciful.

As I write this, I feel joy because I made a decision that was best for me, not my mother, father, or anybody else. I loved myself enough to say, "no" and to trust God. Regardless of where you start, it does not have to be the end. Anyone who is reading this:

- Please get out of those relationships that are causing you pain, turmoil, and separation from God's will.
- Pray and ask God for peace.
- Seek help from loved ones.
- Go to a shelter.
- Write an escape plan. (I remember writing out where I was going, my relevant documents, etc.)
- Tell a trusted friend or counselor for support.
- Love yourself enough to get out!!!

Please don't stay in an abusive situation for the sake of having a relationship or to keep the false peace in a family or any other situation. Abuse is a topic that we as a people (especially in the Christian community) do not like to discuss, but we need to be more transparent and talk about it so we can break the stigmas and deadly cycles. Discussion plus action can be the defining moment for your life and another person's life. "Life and death are in the power of the tongue." Proverbs 18:21. Which one will you choose?

In closing, the following is a testimony poem I wrote last year at a women's retreat. I pray it blesses and encourages those who read to move forward:

LEQUVIA, From Reject to Redeemed

*L*ost in rejection and other's opinions
*E*xpecting love from other people, nothing genuine
*Q*uestioning God's existence and looking for peace
*U*ntil one day, He answered
*V*ictory through Christ Jesus
*I*gnited and set me free
*A*shes of my former self released; I've been redeemed.
Thank you, God. Because you love me, a new
creature in Christ is all I can be.
2 Corinthians 5:17

Aha Moment

Aha Moment

Part Two

"It's Not Whether You Get Knocked Down, It's Whether You Get Up." ~ ~ *Vince Lombardi*

Dreams

Paris Love

I had the most humbling experience. I was in a hospital with a doctor while they were making their rounds. We enter the room of the first patient. The doctor took the bandages from around the patient's head, and the look of horror appeared on her face. The doctor smiled and reassured the patient, "That deafening noise you hear will go away in a minute." And yes, from the look on the patient's face, it did. And the patient was able to hear. Hmm, I thought, how wonderful is it to have the ability to 'hear' after being 'deaf' for an extended period.

I'm not sure of my role here, but the doctor continues to the next patient and takes their bandages off and asked the patient to give it a few minutes. After a few minutes, the patient got up and walk to the wall, looked at it, and said, "Green?" The doctor replied, "Yes." Then the patient went and looked in the full-length mirror, which was on the door I was standing behind. I peeked around so I could see the patient; the doctor is rising to the side observing. The patient looks in the mirror in complete awe all the while touching her face and smiling. I look at the doctor and ask, "Is this the first time, she sees herself." "Yes!" the doctor replied. Wow, how cool is that to be able to see yourself after being blind your entire life? I turn around and cry - I haven't cried like that since I was a child and then I noticed something even more strange. I'm balling, holding my face in my hands, you know that moment when you think "I don't care who sees me cry, you know the ugly face-mouth open, dinosaur tears and snot coming out of your nose" but there are no tears, no snotty nose. Why is that? I'm not 100% sure.

As I awaken, I realized this was just a dream. Perhaps it's related to the events that occurred hours before I retired for the night. See, the day before I went shopping with my mom and tried on a dress, a purple form-fitting sexy knock out dress, but still very appropriate to wear to speak at an event. I try the dress on, look in the full-length mirror. Hmm, cute, but I soon notice the flaws, every curvy bump, the cottage-cheese thighs- and oh how did those thighs get THAT big! I have my mom's knees, my dad's height, and the list goes on. I take the dress off realizing I could pull it off with some spanks but the big question, would I be happy and satisfied wearing it? Probably not. I want to feel sexy wearing the dress, not just look the part.

I stand looking at myself in that full-length mirror in my undies, and my positive, self-loving attitude disappears as I noticed all the flaws, the extra weight, and fat. How did I get here? Why can't I lose the extra pounds? Secretly thankful my sex life is nonexistent, I don't want to see myself and I sure as hell don't want anyone else to see me. Lord, knows I don't.

Before I drift off to sleep, I have a come-to-Jesus conversation with God. Why can't I lose the extra weight? I've been on this quest for a while, and I realized when I was bone thin, I was unhappy with my body, and now I'm even more dissatisfied. Why, why, why. I work out like a madwoman, I watch what I eat, and still, the weight remains. Interesting how you can be on both sides of the spectrum and still not be happy?

After reflecting on the dream, I realized I was the neutral observer, and it's true - how we relate to the issue is the issue. We can't love anyone until we love ourselves. With the right under garments that purple dress would be slamming – but why hide the flaws? Why not embrace them? Yes, we want to be presentable, but when we hide our imperfections, people still see them. No matter how much we smile, tell jokes, educate ourselves, put on makeup, get our hair done. The flaws are still there itching to be seen, embraced, accepted, and loved. After all, it's who we are inside – our imperfections don't define us. They are put there for us to slow down, take notice, and be accountable in how we show up in the world.

Aha Moment

Aha Moment

"Never limit yourself because of others' limited imagination; Never limit others because of your own limited imagination."
~ Mae Jemison

I Like Myself; I Love Myself; I Am My Very Best Friend

Georgia Day

I remember like it was yesterday. My marriage produced two stunningly beautiful daughters – inside and out, but it was beginning to fall apart. Now, we all know it takes two to tango, so I certainly accept responsibility for my mistakes. I thought I had married forever; that was not to be. I was a working mom, with all the pressures that bring to home life. My faith was faltering, and I was spiraling down toward depression. I knew I could not go there; I had two beautiful daughters to support, physically, mentally, emotionally, and spiritually.

So, one day, I was in the bathroom and looked at myself in the mirror – really looked. I had lost a lot of weight, my face was gaunt, and gone was the sunshine smile I had had for a very long time. I stood there, not liking what I saw.

I began to pray, to ask for help, for strength to go on. We had a Jack and Jill bath, and there was a sizeable frosted mirror in the center where the bathtub was located. Suddenly, the sun shone brightly through to my side of the bathroom, hitting the mirror in front of me full force. I was so startled that for a moment, my mind went blank. Then, in my mind, I heard the phrase "I like myself. I love myself. I am my very best friend." I recoiled from the thought at first. Then, I forced the words out of my mouth. Tears began to flow like a river, for what seemed like an eternity. You know, the kind that requires a towel to wipe away.

Continuing to sob, I forced myself to look in the mirror and repeat the message. Slowly my posture improved; I stood straighter, with my head held higher. The words were still crushingly painful, as I did not believe them. It took me a solid month of practicing every day to begin to say them with a smile; to fully believe God would help me through the pain.

And help me, He did! I survived a complicated divorce, struggling to help my daughters through the devastation. In time, I found someone to love my daughters and me, just as we are. I can say that the last 34 years have indeed been a fairy tale. My second marriage has been a treasure of happy memories I will hold in my heart forever. I am grateful for so many things; learning to believe in myself, as a first step in restoring my faith, was indeed a blessing from God.

Aha Moment

Aha Moment

"Here's to strong women.
May we know them.
May we raise them.
May we be them."
~ ~ Anonymous

Motivation and the Role Model
Angela I. Schutz

Zig Ziglar always said that motivation is like bathing; you can't do it just once. I still took that to heart, and so for most of my adult life, I tried to find things that motivated and inspired me. This was especially important to me as I was blundering my way through life. For some reason, if there was a harder way to do things, that's the way, I did them. It wasn't intentional, but it always seemed to be the pattern I followed.

For example, I went away to college right after high school, as is the traditional pattern. I had a great first year if you could say that partying and having fun was what college is all about. By the spring semester, I had to drop out because my grades were so horrible. I went home one weekend and announced to my parents that I was never going back to that school. They said fine. You see, I had an older brother that had gone to five colleges before he finally graduated. My parents made it clear that they were no longer going to pay for college again!

I got a job and eventually got married and had a child. I knew that I would never go to college, and for the most part, I never worried about it again, or so I thought! One day, when my son was twelve, and I was forty, he looked at me and said: "Boy Mom, I hope you get your college degree before I get mine." It was like a knife in my heart. No mother wants to feel her child isn't proud of her. The very next day, I signed up at the local community college and began to earn, and I do mean earn, my college degree.

It wasn't easy because I was working full time, raising a family, and going to school. It was a challenge that, for some reason, I was ready to accept. So I studied, and I studied, and I studied, and I formed study groups, and I made new friends. In the first two years, I earned my Associate's degree. In the next two years, I received my Bachelors' degree, and then I went on to get my Master's degree. In the seventh year since I started this education journey, I was in my last three courses for my Master's degree when I found out I had cancer. Yes, the Big C! That is the thing that fills everyone with fear. The thing we are all convinced will be that which takes us out.

Let me tell you a great lesson I learned when I had cancer. As humans, we don't wear a neon sign on our foreheads that say: I have cancer, or I just got a divorce, or lost a job, or had to bury a loved one. We are tough. It doesn't mean we don't need support, but we don't ask for it. When I thought of that, I realized that every time someone just asked you how you are or pay you an unsolicited compliment, it means so much. I learned that we need to give of ourselves to everyone. Be nice. Pay strangers compliments. Go the distance. That smile you readily give out may be the most beautiful thing a person will experience that entire day.

Well, I had my surgeries, went through treatment, and twenty-three years later, I am fine. There are two results that I have experienced since that time. The first is that because I went back and finished my last three courses after my cancer, I look at my Master's degree as one of the most significant accomplishments in my life. I went on to get much more professional education after that, and now I teach at a local community college.

I have become a role model for each of those students who don't believe they can succeed at college and for those students who think professors and other professionals have had it easy. They look at people who are successful and think they quickly got to that place of success. You can't look at another person and guess what they have been through in life. Many successful people have had to crawl through a lot of mud to get to that place of success. It's the old adage: Never judge a book by its cover.

I went from being a college dropout to being a college professor! I love that I get about 100 opportunities each year to change the mindset of the next generation. I can tell them to be proud of themselves that they are in school and never criticize themselves for starting later than is the traditional pattern. You are ready when you are ready!

As I said, I was really, really good at blundering through life. Another major "bungle" was my marriage. I was raised by parents who ultimately were married for 69 years. They were always happy. I never heard them argue. I never saw them struggle. I figured that I would, of course, have the same kind of life. They were my role models. I missed the message about knowing yourself and picking a life partner who compliments you and will have your back throughout life.

I got married for all the wrong reasons: I was overweight and thought no one would want me; I was getting old and thought no one would want me; I needed to be needed, and so I married a divorced man who was raising his children alone. I am a rescuer by nature. I was so sure I could "fix" their lives and help them.

I never looked for Mr. Right or even Mr. Right Enough. I just settled. It was a horrible relationship, but my catholic upbringing, along with my unwavering sense of loyalty, left me with a 43-year marriage that never should have been. Much of it was toxic, but I told myself that he was the father of my one, amazing son, so I "owed" him my loyalty.

At this point, you might think I am going to say that I am soured on relationships, but I am not. I spent lots of time learning about myself and growing. I learned to be whole and healthy. I learned to appreciate every moment of every day. Now, I am happily dating at the age of 71. I know that there is a life partner out there who will share my values, my dreams, and my desires for the rest of my life. "You are ready when you are ready!"

I have become a role model for other seniors who have previously given up on life. I walk my talk. I have successfully ventured out into the dating world. I have learned so much about the importance of just being yourself and knowing when to walk away from something or someone who doesn't serve you well. Yes, there are some weird people out there. But there are also so many people who have been married and who have loved successfully. They are now alone. They know how to be a good partner. They know how to be reciprocal.

Most importantly, they know that life is short, and every day is precious. They want to journey with someone they can love. They are not strange, and they are just lonely. I have joked that in the dating world, you have to kiss a lot of frogs, but when you kiss the right frog, you will be happier than you have ever been!

I love that I can be a role model for other women, and maybe even some men, who are afraid to date. I tease them and say, let me write your profile. You will get dates! The bottom line is that you can't sit in your house and pine away wishing life was different. You need to take action. When you get onto a dating site, plan on dating, not just becoming someone's pen pal! Don't be rude! Don't ghost people! Don't block people unless they are vulgar or inappropriate to you.

In some cases, technology has created a very unforgiving society. Social skills are fading away, as is grammar, spelling, and patience. With the click of a button, you can eliminate someone from your life forever. What lessons do you learn from that???? If I can motivate even one lonely person to take a leap of faith and look for a new partner with the potential of finding love and happiness, I will be so grateful.

I started down a rocky road as a young woman. I was aimless, clueless, and skilless. Life seemed bleak and often hopeless. I seemed to be going about things in all the wrong ways. One day, I heard an interview with the late Maya Angelou, the famous poet and visionary. She told a story about how, when she was a young woman, she drank too much and smoked too much. She had very little control of herself. She hung around with the wrong people. One day she went to visit her mother. Before she left, her mother told her:" Maya, you were born for greatness."

She left her mother's house, and she started to think about what her mother said. She told herself that if she was born for greatness, she'd better get going! From that point on, after her aha moment in life, she stopped drinking and smoking, and she started to look deep inside herself. She looked for others to motivate her, and she developed a more positive attitude about life. She began to write. She began to philosophize. She began to be the greatness she was meant to be!

As I have traveled down my journey exploring who I was meant to be, I always appreciated Maya Angelou's straightforward, but powerful motivation. We, as humans, are not supposed to be the same. It is genuinely our uniqueness that makes us unique. It is our uniqueness that is so important to the world. Developing that uniqueness is your most important work in life. The world needs you in all your uniqueness and all your glory.

I leave you with the lyrics of a song by Jana Stanfield; "You cannot do all the things that the world needs, but the world needs all the things you can do." Will you dare yourself to go out and do all the things you can do?

Aha Moment

Aha Moment

*"Don't Let Yesterday Take Up
Too Much Of Today."*
~ ~ Will Rogers

Forgiveness (From Beginning to the End)
Monica Fletcher

To seek forgiveness is divine, but to bestow it upon another is like eagerly waiting on a ten-ton boulder to gently thump me in the top of my head! Sounds a bit dramatic? Well, let's pretend, "wink-wink" that I am the only person in the whole wide world who feels that way. And don't even let me find out it was conceived out of malicious intent, oh you get cut off immediately! I think my best separation time is still around 1.3 seconds flat. Family members not excluded. I remember getting mad at my sister when we were kids, simply because she beat me in a foot race. I slammed her butt straight to the ground! Some could say, my poor sister had a slight delay in getting to the emergency room because our momma lit my tale up. I don't know-how in the world she beat me! Y'all, I was a great runner, and everybody in the family knew it too. Thinking back on it, I allowed a childish moment to push me into a cycle of simple unforgiveness, meaning I let my pride get the best of me. I didn't let it go, and so my feelings got the best of me from then on. That day I made a pact with myself to never let anyone get the best of me again. Now, let's talk about an area where forgiveness can get a bit tricky, especially when most days you show up to pay some bills.

Several years ago, I worked for an organization who encouraged employees to labor as independently as possible, while maintaining a team-orientated focus on assigned projects. Of course, there was a catch. We had to agree that should a problem arise; all parties involved would quickly and professionally come up with an amicable resolution. It seemed like a good idea at the time, but it didn't work. Following Luke 16:12 garnered me a total of six workplace friend-a-enemies. You see, I believed God for a family-owned business of my own, but evidently, the co-workers on our team had a different plan for me to follow. Oh, and before I forget those friend-a-enemies, are the folks who can't stand each other, but they will quickly join forces to bring you down. The work atmosphere got so bad that I hated being acknowledged publicly, I don't think I have ever had that many eyes rolling at me at the same time. The more money I was blessed to bring in the tougher it got. Simple questions were emailed to me, and the leadership team was copied in each one. Can't tell you how many times I ask the ring leader of the confusion to meet so that I could find out why they were upset. She turned me down more than once, but I'll never forget the day I received a company award and a member of the team went off! She spoke to someone else but made sure it was loud enough for me to hear, 'Why did she get an award! I been here for years and ain't never got nothing like that.'

Now, know that Jesus in me did not want to pray. I wanted to cuss her out on the spot! We eventually spoke about the incident only to learn that her problem with me (her words not mine) 'You're doing my job,' I asked if she discussed her concerns with management because all the work was assigned to me and of course she shunned that off. I even tried to address the issue with leadership myself and was advised more than once just to keep doing what I was doing. So, I turned to online gospel music, sermons from my pastor, a whole lot of prayer and jokes to get me through the day. Sadly, this toxic atmosphere stayed in place for more than 2 ½ years, and before you ask, yes, I enjoyed my job, giving excellent customer service is the core of who I am. My problem was I had never worked with a group of people who look like me, talked swag like me, getting paid to do the same job as me, but could care less if the work got done.

Of course, I wanted to quit a lot, I mean a whole lot, did I say a lot? I'd go to church or listen to our morning prayer calls, and the message was always the same, 'And I don't know who's dealing with that issue on your job, God told me to tell you just hold on, because it's working it out for your good and His Glory.' I got the same message for more for six months.

Three years in at our annual review, management finally addressed the issue. So here is what I was told, 'I think you should know that the team doesn't trust you, the consensus among the group is that you make them feel like they're not doing a good job.' (Side note, during the workday more than half of their day was spent on social media, chatting with friends on the company's internal networks, shopping for houses, cars for spouses, clothes for kids and wedding favors). Now one could easily assume I would be pissed, but remember I knew this was now a set-up by God and so I asked one question, 'So you're asking me to dumb myself down to be a part of the team?' That room went silent for a full three minutes, and then I was told, don't expect the team to work at the same level as yourself.'

Man, that childhood feeling kicked right on up! Remember my promise? No one was ever going to beat me again, so after that day, so I worked harder. I walked into the office the next morning, and the only words I spoke were, 'Good morning, Good evening.' I didn't talk to anybody unless I absolutely had to and only if it was about work. Well sadly, the foolishness went on for another year, but then one day out of the clear blue the clique, as I began to call the six, emailed a confidential memo to the new senior management about their job displeasure and of course I was still the antagonist of the story. But guess who was included in the complaint this time? Yep, Mr. Annual Reviewer himself! I mean they went all in even accusing him of letting me run the department without the position of course. A strange thing happened, when the first complaint fell on deaf ear, they wrote a second one three months later.

So here is the irony of the story, the more they lashed out at me, I began to get these overwhelming urges to pray for them. Moral of the story, the people did not change nor the situation but one day on my way to work I did something that I felt wasn't even necessary for me to do, but I did it anyway. I forgave each one of them. And that day, it hit me that it took me from age 10 to age 44 to finally get what God was trying to show me. Of course, I got a ton of unforgiveness stories, but this is where it all started for me. It took me a long time to accept Matthew 6:15 from the Holy Bible, but if ye forgive not men their trespasses, neither will your Father forgive your trespasses. I had to let it go to be forgiven for my stuff.

Aha Moment

Aha Moment

"You are confined only by the walls you build yourself."
~ ~ *Andrew Murphy*

About the Authors

Paris Love
Author, Speaker, Organizational and Productivity Consultant

Paris Love, CEO of the Paris Love Productivity Institute is *the* country's foremost organizational and productivity coaches. Love is a former U.S. Army Sergeant, who has a tremendous talent for bringing order to chaos, providing her clients with streamlined, efficient, manageable approaches to running their lives and businesses.

Love says, "It is not about the clutter, it is about something else" and she is good at ascertaining what that 'something else' is. With a knack for identifying the emotional and physical clutter and a gift for crafting useful, practical solutions, Love has helped individuals and companies of all sizes get organized and on track to living a stress-free life. Her energetic, no-nonsense approach, combined with her ability to produce immediate results, appeals to individuals, high-powered CEOs and small business professionals alike.

Paris is also the creator of the SPARK Retreat where she helps spirit-minded women overcome obstacles, and limiting beliefs so they can stand in their power and live the life they crave. Learn more at https://parisloveinstitute.com.

Glenda F. Woodard
Financial Management Officer, Retired

Ms. Glenda Faye Woodard is a Financial Management Officer who retired from the United States Air Force in December 2012. She managed an annual operating Budget for the 403rd Wing, Air Force Reserve, Keesler Air Force Base, Mississippi. The budget totaled over $100M, which included funds for Operations and Maintenance, Reserve Personnel and Military Personnel Appropriations.

Ms. Woodard was born in Birmingham, Alabama, and graduated from Westfield High School. She attended Southern Jr. College of Business, Birmingham, Al; Major, Business Administration; Compton Jr. College, Compton, California, Major, Nursing; Mississippi Gulf Coast Community College, Major, Business Administration. She also completed several Air Force training courses to include, Base Level Stock Fund Management, Denver CO; Introduction to Base Civil Engineering, Air University, Air Force Institute of Technology, Wright Patterson AFB, OH; Seven Habits of Highly Effective People, Keesler AFB, MS.

Ms. Woodard began her Federal Service career in Neu Ulm, Germany, 1979. She transferred back to the United States in 1980 and continued her Federal Service career promoted through the ranks from GS-3 to GS-13. Ms. Woodard held positions as Supply Clerk, Suggestion Clerk, Assistant Stock Fund Manager, Financial Analyst, and Financial Management Officer. She received numerous awards: 1982, Civilian of the Quarter; 1987, Outstanding United States Air Force Supply Technician; 1989, Outstanding United States Air Force Supply Supervisor of the Year; 1990, Civilian Woman of the Year; 1991, Civilian of the Quarter; 1993, Certificate of Appreciation from Mayor of Biloxi; 1995, Headquarter Air Force Reserve Command Financial Analyst of the Year; 2005, Certificate, Grief Share Leader, Brentwood Baptist Church, Brentwood, TN; 2007, Certificate, Stephen Series Leader's Training Course, Corpus Christi, TX; 209, Certified

Facilitator, 7 Habits of Highly Effective People; 2011, Headquarters Air Force Reserve Command Financial Analysis Office of the Year Award.

Ms. Woodard sponsors three children through World Vision International and two children through Compassion International and is a Partner in Hope with St. Jude Children's Hospital.

She is a member of the National Association of Professional Woman (NAPW) and a Mary Kay Consultant. Her hobbies include reading Inspirational books, gardening, listening to Christian Contemporary and Gospel music, and interior decorating. She has one daughter who graduated from Rice University, Houston, TX, with a BS in Civil Engineering and from the University of Pennsylvania - Wharton College with an MBA.

Georgia Day
President, Kamama LLC

As I reflect on my years in business, I have worked in many areas. I spent time in private industry before developing a career in the public sector. During this time, I served on numerous boards and commissions, both nationally and locally. My husband Michael and I then began our next life chapter, spending ten years working and traveling full time across the country in our RV, later settling in Austin, TX.

As a Career Success & Fulfillment Coach, author, and speaker, I help professionals in the corporate area get to that next successful step in their careers. I also work with those who have forgotten, or don't even believe that they can have a life outside of the business. They may feel overwhelmed and trapped, with no real personal time, or have lost the ability to make their dreams a reality. I work with them to create practical, workable solutions in both areas of their lives. I do not take this privilege lightly.

My heartfelt gratitude goes to my clients, who have achieved success in ways that empower and sustain them, and I am fortunate to have been a part of that journey.

Visit https://www.amazon.com/author/georgiaday for a list of publications

Angela I. Schutz

Angela I. Schutz is Managing Director/Founder of Driven To Succeed Consulting LLC, a career development/executive coaching and public speaking service aimed at empowering people to find their ultimate career potential. Her coaching success includes helping more than two hundred of her clients land jobs in a two and a half year period, dispelling the myth that "there are no jobs out there"!

Angela's career includes serving as a virtual coach for CareerCurve; as a Certified Associate at Lee Hecht Harrison and as a University Relations Career Consultant, coaching MBA and EMBA students; she served as the Executive Director of Training and Development for the National Society of Leadership and Success; and held multiple positions at the University of New Haven such as: the Director of Career Services and Experiential Learning, the Director to the Program to China and the Assistant Dean for Academic Services.

Angela earned her B.A. in Psychology at Southern Connecticut State University. She completed her graduate work at the University of New Haven where she earned an M.A. in Community Psychology. She is a qualified Myers-Briggs Type Indicator Administrator and holds a Management Certificate in Higher Education from the Higher Education Resource Service (HERS) at Wellesley College.

Angela is trained by Jack Canfield, author of the Success Principles and numerous Chicken Soup for the Soul books, Marcia Wieder, Founder and CEO of Dream University and Tory Johnson, Founder and CEO of Women for Hire, the premier career organization in America for women.

Kimberly J. Sharkey

Kimberly J. Sharkey was born and raised on the Southside of Chicago. She attended George Washington Carver, a Performing Arts School. Kimberly embraced the counsel of a teacher to take up journalism and participated in a summer program where she was able to intern with the Jet Magazine. She later went on the attend Southern Illinois University in Carbondale, earning a Bachelor of Science in Workforce Education and Development with a specialty in Curriculum Development and an Associates in Human Services.

She relocated to Atlanta, Georgia after college and started her career at Hartsfield-Jackson International airport. She's worked in several business units over the last 20 years. She's currently seeking to complete the Project Management certification as she constantly takes on educational goals to meet her desire to ever evolve through learning.

She's the author of *Seasons of Intentional Relationships*, penned in 2014 and working on her second book, *"Open Up: You Have to Write to Tell Your Story,"* Kimberly is a minister who started a writer's support group and brought the attention for the need of a Scribal Ministry at New Birth Missionary Baptist Church in Stonecrest. She embarked upon being an entrepreneur with her innovative and nontraditional and unconventional publishing company, Global enterUPtion, Literary Group. To date, she has published four projects.

She's a sought out international speaker, sharing her witty, down-to-earth, thought-provoking and an intentional message about family, relationships, and faith. She knows that everyone has a story to tell, and it unfolds when you encounter her. You can contact Kimberly at www.kimberlyjsharkey.com

Monica Martin Fletcher

Monica Martin Fletcher, a relationship author who lives in Atlanta, Georgia with her spouse Michael, and host of her own weekly online Facebook video chat entitled, Lunch Time Love Moments, where she tackles the subject, *Teach Me to How to Date, Not to Cohabit.* Her first book, *The Shacking Diaries,* available at Smashwords, allowed Monica to interview several women about their personal cohabitation experiences. In her most recent title, *'Just Sex' Is Not A Relationship,* available on Amazon, helps to bridge the conversational gap about shacking up and how to break the generational soul-ties to it.

Author Monica Martin Fletcher is just a southern-born Christian girl who thought life would be far less complicated when she ran away from home at the ripe old age of eighteen. Unfortunately, a journey that took more than twenty-five years did not go as planned but rest assured the experience was undoubtedly her destined path. Armed with a heart of rage and a trail of broken excuses not to forget or to forgive, one night she grabbed the Holy Bible, a pen and a pad and started to write any and everything thing that was hidden on the inside. At the end of the night, her tears reminded her how important it is for women to express those blindfolded feelings even when it does feel right. Living within the headspace of a six-year-old little girl was tricky.

To learn more about Monica's story, check out her website at www.monicamartinfletcher.com.

Brittany Lorenzi

With 20 years of finance and operations experience, and a healthy dose of business acumen. Brittany Lorenzi has used her passion for helping entrepreneurs grow their businesses to fuel the meteoric rise of BluePrint Strategy and Collaborate | An Entrepreneurial Community.

A native of Louisville, KY, Brittany's love for entrepreneurship and real estate was heavily influenced by her parents, both entrepreneurs in the field. So, it seemed inevitable that she would follow in their footsteps. But few would imagine she'd do it before the ink dried on her college degree.

While working toward a BA in Business at Hanover College, Brittany took a little swatch of land that her parents gifted her next to an office building and transformed it into a paid parking lot. Still sensing an opportunity, she convinced the owners of the office building to let her put a vending machine in the lobby. Her efforts paid off. In addition to the income, she generated from parking fees and snack foods. Brittany was awarded the State of Indiana Collegiate Entrepreneur Award for her excellence in business development, strategy, and execution.

The experience gave Brittany her first real taste of how it felt to bring an idea to market. She also learned the importance of financing.

Brittany's career trajectory leads her into commercial real estate and executive-level financial positions. It was her success as one of five founders of a Nashville-based commercial real estate firm – with revenue upwards of $8MM, 75 employees, and three different locations. That solidified her place as a results-driven business strategist, commercial real estate maven, and calculated risk-taker.

After selling her share in the commercial real estate firm, Brittany launched BluePrint Strategy. She is offering business solutions designed to help companies grow, from strategic planning and business modeling to back-office support. And through her new initiative, Collaborate | An Entrepreneurial Community. She meets the physical needs of businesses, giving them a place to work in a professional setting, learning from and sharing with like-minded individuals with a common goal: building a successful business.

For some, achieving such success would make them inaccessible. But for Brittany, the opposite is true. A member of the Entrepreneurs' Organization, Brittany enjoys mentoring other women on the importance of funding their business, mapping a thriving strategy to grow that business, and managing the ebbs and flows of business ownership. "Many businesses fail due to lack of proper funding and poor planning. You have to invest in your company, persevere, and hold yourself accountable," says Brittany. "Running a business is a roller coaster ride. Early on, I didn't even realize how steep the ups and downs could be." She continues, "But it's the best ride you'll ever be on."

Lequvia K. Ousley

Lequvia K. Ousley is a native of Dawson, GA and a graduate of Terrell County High School. Lequvia has an A.S. in Business Administration from Darton College, B.S. in Accounting from Albany State University, a Master's in Accounting and Financial Management from Keller Graduate School of Management, and pursuing a Master's in Professional Writing at Liberty University.

It was at the age of 13 when Lequvia was given a diary that she fell in love with writing. Growing up in a sheltered environment, Lequvia always felt she didn't have a voice. Writing for Lequvia was therapeutic and an escape from her surroundings. After graduating and moving to Atlanta in 2008, the personal blogs and journal writing slowly stopped, as Lequvia began her career in accounting. It wasn't until 2012 that Lequvia started to miss her love of writing and blogging. While working as a staff accountant, Lequvia noticed that her knack for writing and proofreading were evident. In July of 2012, she began working as a guest blogger for ROAR, a nonprofit birthed from a church member, whose focus was on educating students and the community on various resources for success. It was during this assignment that Lequvia noticed her writing take a different direction. Her posts were a combination of practicality and spirituality. She utilized personal experiences from school and college to create posts that were inspirational to readers. Before she writes, she always asks God to give her the content to write. It was in those moments that she realized that writing was a gift God gave her to help others.

While attending graduate school, Lequvia decided to create two personal blogs with blog platforms, Blogger & Tumblr as a way to relieve stress. As the demands of the class took over, Lequvia began to withdraw further from her writing. It wasn't until her accounting job ended in 2013, that she decided to explore her gift of writing and connect with others who shared the same passion. As of 2014, she currently maintains her blog, DivineGift317: (http://divinegift317.blogspot.com) and is the blogmaster for The Write Moment (http://thewritemoment1.blogspot.

com), a blog associated with Just Write, a writer's support group birthed through the EICC (Embassy International Chamber of Commerce) ARTS ministry. It was through Just Write's support, accountability, and encouragement of fellow writers, where she became inspired to launch a business to help others.

In addition to being an experienced accounting and administrative professional, Lequvia is also a former math study skills teacher/online tutor, and current freelance writer/blogger who loves to create and edit content for others through her business, D.I.V.I.N.E. Blogger, LLC, a business specializing in "Developing Intellectual Visionaries Individual Needs Exceptionally" through writing, editing, blogging, and social media services. When she is not tackling administrative/writing tasks for her peers and clients, Lequvia is passionate about learning new things, serving in her church and community, and donating to her favorite organizations. A self-proclaimed introverted extrovert, Lequvia loves purple, butterflies, new experiences (food or travel), reading a great book, listening to her favorite old school tunes, enjoying a great movie or discussion, and connecting with family and friends. Lequvia's motto is "Success is the positive result of using one's God-given gifts to serve others."

For more information, please connect with Lequvia at www. lequviakousley.com.

THE KENNEDY AUTOPSY